NATURAL CLEANING

NATURAL CLEANING

DIY Solutions for the Kitchen, Bedroom, Bathroom, Office, and More

Pam Farley

brownthumbmama.com

Skyhorse Publishing

Skyhorse Publishing books may be purchased in bulk at special discounts for sales promotion, corporate gifts, fund-raising, or educational purposes. Special editions can also be created to specifications. For details, contact the Special Sales Department, Skyhorse Publishing, 307 West 36th Street, 11th Floor, New York, NY 10018 or info@skyhorsepublishing.com.

Skyhorse® and Skyhorse Publishing® are registered trademarks of Skyhorse Publishing, Inc.®, a Delaware corporation.

Visit our website at www.skyhorsepublishing.com.

10 9 8 7 6 5 4 3 2 1

Library of Congress Cataloging-in-Publication Data
Names: Farley, Pam, author.
Title: Natural cleaning : DIY solutions for the kitchen, bedroom, bathroom,
   office, and more / Pam Farley, BrownThumbMama.com.
Description: New York : Skyhorse Publishing, [2022] | Includes index. |
   Summary: "Protect your health, reduce waste, and be a better steward of
   the Earth by making the switch to natural cleaning products with these
   43 easy recipes"-- Provided by publisher.
Identifiers: LCCN 2022013762 (print) | LCCN 2022013763 (ebook) | ISBN
   9781510771482 (paperback) | ISBN 9781510771499 (epub)
Subjects: LCSH: House cleaning. | Natural products. | Formulas, recipes,
   etc.
Classification: LCC TX324 .F36 2022 (print) | LCC TX324 (ebook) | DDC
   648/.5--dc23/eng/20220416
LC record available at https://lccn.loc.gov/2022013762
LC ebook record available at https://lccn.loc.gov/2022013763

Cover design by David Ter-Avanesyan
Cover and interior images courtesy of Shutterstock
Interior design and layout by Chris Schultz

Print ISBN: 978-1-5107-7148-2
Ebook ISBN: 978-1-5107-7149-9

Printed in China

TABLE OF CONTENTS

INTRODUCTION

Welcome to *Natural Cleaning*! This is an introduction to homemade, natural cleaners for everyone who cares about the health of their body and the planet.

My name is Pam Farley, and I've been cleaning my house with a few basic, natural ingredients for more than twenty-five years. I've learned a lot about what works and even more about what doesn't work.

In *Natural Cleaning*, I'll explain why these cleaners work, and discuss why you shouldn't use some DIY cleaning recipes you see online. Things like:

- Why you shouldn't mix vinegar and castile soap
- Why you should use purified water instead of tap water
- How to customize your cleaners with essential oils

You can read this book straight through from beginning to end or use the table of contents to skip from one section to another as needed.

Happy cleaning!

WHY MAKE THE SWITCH TO NATURAL CLEANING?

Switching to natural cleaning methods just makes sense. There are tons of benefits and no downsides!

Safety Is #1

Common household cleaners are not kid-friendly or pet-friendly. Store-bought cleaners like bleach, ammonia, drain cleaners, toilet cleaners, and more are the cause of thousands of household emergencies each year[*].

These are strong chemicals that can cause irritation, burns, and poisoning. Your home is simply safer without them.

Cleaner Air

The biggest thing I noticed when I made the switch to natural cleaning was improved air quality. The harsh cleaners with artificial fragrances irritated my airways and gave me headaches.

These symptoms cleared up the moment I switched to making my own cleaners. If you have asthma or allergies, natural cleaning is even more important.

Save Money

Nothing makes me happier than finding budget-friendly ways to stay healthy. Basic natural cleaning ingredients are easy to find, and the finished products are much cheaper

---

[*]   Lara B. McKenzie, Nisha Ahir, Uwe Stolz, and Nicolas G. Nelson. "Household Cleaning Product-Related Injuries Treated in US Emergency Departments in 1990-2006." *Pediatrics*. U.S. National Library of Medicine. Accessed December 17, 2021. pubmed.ncbi.nlm.nih.gov/20679298/.

than buying prepackaged products. Plus, if you run out of a cleaner you can make another batch without a trip to the store.

When you switch to DIY cleaning products, you'll save money while making your home a safer place.

Fewer Products

Did you know that you don't actually need a different cleaner for every surface in your house? Seriously! All those bottles of conventional cleaners equal wasted money and materials. All you really need are a few basic supplies and ingredients to clean every part of your home.

BASIC NATURAL CLEANING INGREDIENTS

So, what ingredients do you need to get started? Here's what you'll find most useful:

Baking Soda

For scouring and deodorizing, you can't beat baking soda. You can get a jumbo-sized box for just a few dollars.

Baking soda is alkaline, so it makes soap more effective. Baking soda + castile soap is the winning combo for scrubbing away dirt and grime.

White Vinegar

A gallon of white vinegar is inexpensive, will last for ages, and is useful in many areas of the home. It cuts through tough buildup from hard water and soap scum because it's acidic.

If you don't like the smell of vinegar, make infused vinegar with citrus peels.

To make infused vinegar, peel the rind (not the white pith) from your favorite citrus fruits. You can use a single type, or a combination. I like to use grapefruit vinegar in the bathroom, and lemon-orange vinegar in the kitchen.

Place the peels in a clean glass jar and pour white vinegar over the top to fill the jar. Put a lid on the jar and let it steep for about a week.

Strain off the peels and use them to freshen your garbage disposal. Then label the jar and use your citrus vinegar in any cleaning recipe that calls for white vinegar.

Note: because vinegar is acidic, don't use it on porous surfaces like granite, marble, or natural stone.

Castile Soap

Castile soap is highly effective for breaking down dirt, grime, and grease. It's safe for kids and pets, too. It's made from natural vegetable oils and lye (as opposed to other soaps traditionally made with animal fat, like tallow).

The name comes from the Castile region in Spain, which is famous for its olive oil soaps. Today, castile soap is made from olive oil and a variety of other oils.

You can get castile soap in a bar or liquid form, and I use both types. I like bar soap for handwashing and showers and use unscented liquid castile soap for most DIY recipes.

Distilled or Purified Water

It's important to use distilled water or water that's been purified in a Berkey Filter for these recipes.

Tap water (and well water) contains microorganisms, bacteria, viruses, pharmaceuticals, lead, chemicals, and more. If you make the recipes in this book with tap water, you're spraying these contaminants all over your home!

You can look up your water quality using the Environmental Working Group's Tap Water Database (ewg.org/tapwater). Be warned, though—you might not like what you read.

Yes, there are federal requirements for water quality. However, as we've seen from the conditions in Flint, Michigan, these are not always maintained.

Purified water is a step above filtered water. Filters remove most bacteria, lead, and chemicals. They also remove the chlorine that's used to treat tap water, as well as any particulates that cause water to have taste or odor (eeeew).

Berkey water purifiers do all of these things **plus** remove at least 99.9999 percent of pathogenic bacteria and reduce viruses by 99.99 percent. Impressive, yes?

We use purified water from our Berkey Filter for drinking, cooking, and cleaning. You can absolutely taste the difference when your water is clean and pure, and I feel much better when my family's water is completely and truly clean.

You can learn more about Berkey Water Filters at brownthumbmama.com/best-water -filter.

Essential Oils

Artificial fragrances are one of the main reasons I avoid store-bought cleaners. Instead, I use essential oils to add scents to my cleaning recipes.

Essential oils are extracted from plant parts (roots, stems, leaves, and flowers) and are carefully curated to preserve the potent properties of the oil. When you use essential oils for cleaning, you are relying on the natural chemical components found in the oil to provide cleansing and purifying power.

When used carefully, essential oils can be an important part of your natural cleaning routine. They are very concentrated, so you only need a few drops. When buying essential oils, look for quality brands that don't include fillers or artificial ingredients. You can see my recommendations in my Amazon store: amazon.com/shop/brown thumbmama.

Each essential oil recommended in this book has a unique set of chemical compounds that give the oil specific cleaning benefits. Citrus essential oils like lemon and orange help bust through grease, grime, and sticky messes. Tea tree, thyme, and rosemary purify while eliminating odors.

Essential oils also add aromatherapy benefits, which means you can reduce stress while you clean. (Who would have thought?)

Rubbing Alcohol

For glass, granite, and any other surface that needs to shine, you just need a little rubbing alcohol. Alcohol gives things that "squeaky clean" we all know and love without the toxic fumes of ammonia and other harsh cleaners. It's also safe for porous surfaces like granite and marble.

NATURAL CLEANING TOOLS & SUPPLIES

While the ingredients you use are important, so are proper cleaning tools. When you have the right supplies on hand, it makes cleaning easier and more effective.

Here are the main supplies you'll need for these recipes:

Sixteen-Ounce or Larger Spray Bottles

I prefer glass spray bottles because glass is eco-friendly and easier to wash. However, if your kids help you clean (another advantage of using safe, natural cleaners!) then you might want to use plastic spray bottles.

Microfiber Cleaning Cloths

As you can tell from the name, microfiber cloths are made with tiny, tiny fibers. This means that they are very absorbent, durable, and attract more dirt than conventional cloths. They can be washed and reused for years, which makes them very inexpensive over time. To avoid cross contamination, use different colors for different rooms.

Sturdy Scrub Brush

A wooden scrub brush with natural bristles is the most eco-friendly choice. Once it's worn out, you can safely add it to your compost bin for complete recycling.

THE DIFFERENCE BETWEEN SOAP & DETERGENT

What's the difference between soap and detergent? And why does it matter? The short answer is: soap is natural and detergent isn't. But there's more to it than that.

How Soap Is Made

Soap is created by mixing fats and oils with an alkali or base. This method has been around for hundreds of years—remember the soft soap Ma used in the Little House books? It was created with ashes (that contain lye, a base) with animal fats.

You can use commercial-grade lye, oils, and colorants to make homemade soap. Because we have little ones, and lye is caustic and dangerous, I prefer to make soap without using lye. It's a fun project to do with the kids, and you can scent it with the essential oils or herbs of your choice.

Because soap is natural, it is biodegradable and less harmful to the environment than detergents. However, the minerals in water react with soap and can turn clothes gray and leave a film or residue. Detergent is a big improvement, as far as laundry is concerned!

How Detergent Is Made

Detergents are made by combining chemicals in a slurry mixer. The mixture heats up as a result of chemical reactions, and then it's dried and powdered to form the final product. On average, there are about ten steps between the original raw materials and the final detergent.

If you're using a liquid detergent, then it's probably had water added to it after it was dried and powdered. Crazy, huh?

However: because detergents don't react as much with the minerals in water, they're the best choice for laundry.

How to Tell the Difference

It's confusing because most detergents are camouflaged as soaps. Manufacturers use the terms "facial bar" and "body cleansing bar" to keep us guessing.

How can you tell them apart? Read the label.

Look for chemicals like sodium lauryl sulfate or cocomidopropyl betaine, and then run the other way. True soaps have ingredients like oils, saponified oils, or glycerin.

Soaps and detergent are used on our skin, our clothes, and in our homes. Immediately after use, they go down the drain and into our environment.

Doesn't it make sense to use the least toxic products we can find?

KITCHEN

For most families, the kitchen is where the action is. It's where we spend most of our time: cooking, eating, working, doing homework, and much more. So of course, the kitchen is where lots of messes happen. It's easy to tackle even the toughest kitchen problems with these homemade cleaners and keep dangerous chemicals out of your kitchen.

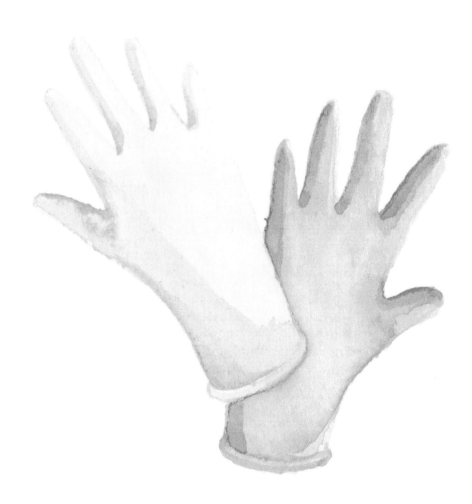

All-Purpose Cleaner

· ·

No need to try 409 different cleaner recipes—this one is fantastic! (Sorry, I couldn't help myself.)

This all-purpose cleaner cuts grease and is great for cleaning just about every kitchen surface. Don't use it on marble or granite, though, because the vinegar is acidic and can damage the stone.

Ingredients

½ cup white vinegar or citrus vinegar

1 teaspoon Dr. Bronner's Sal Suds

15 drops tea tree essential oil

1½ cups distilled or purified water

Supplies

16-ounce spray bottle

Instructions

• Add all your ingredients to your spray bottle in the order listed. Label the bottle, shake gently to mix, and start cleaning.

Note

• This recipe calls for Dr. Bronner's Sal Suds instead of castile soap. There's an important reason for this. Many DIY cleaner recipes mix vinegar and castile soap, but this is *not* a good idea. Here's why, according to the good folks at Dr. Bronner's: the vinegar will cause the castile soap to "unsaponify" and you'll have curds in your cleaner. Ick.

Granite Cleaner

. . . .

Because granite is a porous stone, it's important not to use acidic cleaners containing vinegar. Those cleaners can strip the sealant, making your granite countertop more likely to be stained. This easy recipe cleans while keeping the sealant intact.

Ingredients

¼ cup rubbing alcohol

5 drops unscented liquid castile soap

Distilled or purified water

Supplies

16-ounce spray bottle

Instructions

- Pour the rubbing alcohol and castile soap into the spray bottle, then add water to fill. Shake gently to combine and label the bottle.

To Use

- Spray on your counters and use a clean microfiber cloth to wipe.

Stainless Steel Cleaner

Stainless steel appliances are sleek and modern, but oh boy do they show fingerprints and smudges. There's no need to buy expensive stainless steel cleaner when you can make your own for less.

Ingredients

1 cup white vinegar or citrus vinegar

½ cup distilled or purified water

10 drops lemon or orange essential oil, optional

Supplies

16-ounce spray bottle

Instructions

- First check your owner's manual to make sure your appliance does not have an oil-repellent coating, because the vinegar will remove this coating.

- Put the vinegar, water, and essential oil (if using) in the spray bottle. Swirl to combine and label the bottle.

To Use

- When cleaning, look at the direction of the grain on the appliance. The lines will either be horizontal or vertical. Spray the cleaner and wipe the same way as the grain. Don't scrub crossways, or you'll damage the finish. Wipe all excess cleaner away and don't let it run down the surface of the appliance.

Glass Cleaner

. . . .

The blue glass cleaner we all grew up with is full of chemicals that don't belong in our homes—things like 2-Hexoxyethanol, isopropanolamine, sodium dodecylbenzene sulfonate, lauramine oxide, and lots more.

These chemicals are so nasty that the Environmental Working Group gave this glass cleaner a health grade of "D."[*] These ingredients have the potential to cause acute aquatic toxicity, negative respiratory effects, and negative nervous system effects.

This natural glass cleaner can be used on windows, mirrors, glass, and faucets. It only costs pennies to make and doesn't contain ammonia like some other DIY recipes.

Ingredients

1 cup rubbing alcohol

1 tablespoon white vinegar or citrus vinegar

Distilled or purified water

Supplies

16-ounce spray bottle

Instructions

* Pour the rubbing alcohol and vinegar into the spray bottle and fill with water. Label the bottle, shake gently, and start spraying!

To Use

* When cleaning windows, mirrors, shower doors, and other glass surfaces, always wipe from top to bottom. This prevents drips and streaks. Spray thoroughly and wipe dry with a clean microfiber cloth.

---

[*] "Windex Advanced Glass & Multi-Surface Cleaner Cleaner Rating." EWG's Guide to Healthy Cleaning. Accessed December 23, 2021. ewg.org/guides/cleaners/1418-WindexAdvanced GlassMulti-SurfaceCleaner.

Oven Cleaner

· ·

Cleaning the oven is a pain! I don't have one of those fancy self-cleaning models—mine requires elbow grease to get clean.

Ease away from those chemical cleaners and use this natural combo for a one-two cleaning punch.

Mix this two-part recipe up as needed—don't try to store it for later.

Ingredients

½ cup table salt

¼ cup borax

2 cups baking soda

¾ cup white vinegar or citrus vinegar

20 drops lemon or orange essential oil

Supplies

16-ounce spray bottle

Instructions

- Put the salt, borax, and baking soda in a large bowl. Break up any lumps with a whisk or fork. Add water to form a thick paste.

To Use

- Spread the paste on the oven floor and walls (not the window) and allow it to sit for 20–30 minutes.
- Add the vinegar and essential oil to the spray bottle and gently swirl to combine.
- Spray this mixture over the paste (it will bubble) and wipe away/scrub as needed.
- Use steel wool to easily scrub away any tough spots.
- Using a clean microfiber cloth or sponge, wipe the oven thoroughly clean so no residue remains.

Scouring Powder

Homemade scouring powder was one of the easiest changes to make when I switched to natural cleaners. It works great, is safe around kids and pets, and you probably have all the ingredients in your pantry right now.

The commonly used scouring powder in the green can is so unhealthy that the Environmental Working Group gave it a health grade of "D."[*] It contains ingredients with potential for human respiratory damage, as well as immediate and long-term danger to aquatic creatures. Yikes!

Ingredients

1 cup baking soda

¼ cup table salt

15 drops lemon essential oil

Supplies

Jar with shaker lid (a powdered Parmesan cheese shaker works great)

Instructions

- Put the baking soda and salt in a large bowl. Break up any lumps with a whisk or fork.
- Sprinkle the lemon essential oil on top and whisk again to distribute throughout the baking soda and salt mixture.
- Pour into a jar with a shaker lid and label the jar clearly.

To Use

- Sprinkle on soiled areas and scrub with a damp microfiber cloth or sponge.

---

[*] "Comet Disinfectant Cleanser Powder with Bleach Cleaner Rating." EWG. Accessed December 23, 2021. ewg.org/guides/cleaners/2228-CometDisinfectantCleanserPowderwithBleach/.

Corian Stain Remover

....

Corian, or solid-surface counters, are sturdy, heat-resistant, and scratchproof. These are great qualities, but if your sink gets a rust stain it's very hard to clean (ask me how I know).

This combo removes stains without using bleach or strong chemicals. We have a white sink, so it didn't affect the color, but if you have a colored sink, test it in a hidden area first to be sure.

Mix this recipe up as needed—don't try to store it for later.

Ingredients

¼ cup baking soda

2–3 tablespoons hydrogen peroxide

Instructions

- Mix baking soda and hydrogen peroxide together to make a paste.

To Use

- Spread onto the stain and let it sit for up to 24 hours. Scrub gently while rinsing and repeat if needed.

Kitchen Sink Scrub

This scrubbing liquid works the same as scouring powder but is easier to use on curved surfaces like sinks and the edges of pans.

Ingredients

2 tablespoons unscented liquid castile soap

¾ cup baking soda

2–3 tablespoons purified or distilled water

10 drops lemon or orange essential oil, optional

Supplies

Squeeze bottle (a recycled ketchup bottle works well)

Instructions

- Put the castile soap and baking soda in a small bowl, and whisk to remove any lumps. Add the essential oil, if using, and enough water to make a thin paste.

- Pour into the squeeze bottle and label.

To Use

- Put a small amount onto a damp sponge or microfiber cloth and scrub. Rinse well.

Garbage Disposal Tabs

Is your kitchen sink smelly? It happens to everybody when junk gets caught in the garbage disposal blades. These garbage disposal cleaning tabs are perfect for those times when your sink needs a quick fix.

Ingredients

1 cup baking soda

½ cup table salt

4 tablespoons lemon juice

20 drops lemon essential oil

Supplies

Silicone mold or ice cube tray

Instructions

- Put the baking soda and salt in a large bowl. Break up any lumps with a whisk or fork.

- Mix in the lemon juice and lemon essential oil. The mixture will begin clumping and will stick together slightly.

- Transfer the mixture into ice cube trays or a silicone mold and press down until each compartment is hard packed with the mixture.

- Allow to dry completely for 12–24 hours. When they are thoroughly dry, remove them from the trays and store them in a container with a tight-fitting lid.

To Use

- With the water running, toss one tab in the garbage disposal and run until completely dissolved. Continue running the water for 30 seconds afterward to flush everything through the pipes.

Liquid Dish Soap

. . . .

There are a lot of homemade dish soap recipes online, but many of them don't lather and don't cut grease. That's because they're using soap instead of detergent—and there are some applications for which soap won't do the trick.

This easy recipe lathers up nicely, and cuts grease because of the vinegar and the lemon essential oil. The kosher salt helps the mixture thicken to the consistency we're used to with dish soap.

Ingredients

½ cup Dr. Bronner's Sal Suds

½ cup white vinegar or citrus vinegar

½ cup warm purified or distilled water

1 tablespoon kosher salt

20 drops lemon, orange, or grapefruit essential oil

Supplies

Squeeze bottle (an upcycled ketchup or dish soap bottle is perfect)

Instructions

- Combine the Sal Suds, vinegar, and distilled water and whisk to combine. Add the kosher salt and stir until it thickens; then add essential oils.

- Pour into the squeeze bottle, label clearly, and tell the kids it's time to wash the dishes.

Kitchen Cabinet Cleaner

. . . .

Kitchen cabinets get a lot of abuse—from kids' sticky fingers, cooking grease, spills, and more. If cleaning cabinets isn't part of your regular routine, all the dirt and grime will build up and they can be tough to clean.

This mixture cleans with castile soap and degreases with lemon essential oil, to get your cabinets back to their original, shiny state.

Ingredients

2 tablespoons unscented liquid castile soap

5 drops lemon essential oil

1 cup hot tap water

Instructions

- Mix all ingredients in a small bowl. Wash cabinets with a microfiber cloth.

Fruit & Vegetable Wash

It's always a good idea to wash your fruits and vegetables before eating or cooking. Washing produce helps remove bacteria, pesticide residue, and the food-grade wax that's applied to many vegetables and fruits.

Ingredients

Unscented liquid castile soap

Lemon essential oil

Instructions

- Add 1 teaspoon of castile soap and 2–3 drops of lemon essential oil per gallon of warm water in the sink.
- Add produce and soak for 1–2 minutes, then swish gently to loosen dirt and debris. Rinse with cool water and your produce is clean!

Dishwasher Detergent

Many homemade dishwasher detergent recipes can leave a white film on plates and glasses. This two-part recipe uses citric acid powder and vinegar to help prevent this film from forming.

Ingredients

2 cups washing soda

2 cups borax

6 tablespoons citric acid powder

30 drops lemon or orange essential oil

White vinegar or citrus vinegar

Supplies

Large canning jar or other airtight container

Instructions

- In a large bowl, mix the washing soda, borax, and citric acid powder. Break up any lumps with a whisk or fork. Add the essential oil and mix again with whisk or fork to combine.

- Do not add the vinegar to this mixture! Store in an airtight container.

To Use

- Put 2 tablespoons per load into the dishwasher soap dispenser. Fill the rinse aid section with vinegar and run the dishwasher on the hottest cycle your dishes can handle.

Naturally Clean Your Dishwasher

Automatic dishwashers work hard, and they need to be cleaned occasionally to remove grime, dissolve mineral deposits, and eliminate odors. Cleaning your dishwasher every few months will help it work more efficiently and solve or prevent any drainage problems.

Ingredients

White vinegar or citrus vinegar

Baking soda

Supplies

Toothpicks

Old toothbrush

Medical gloves, optional

Instructions

- Remove the bottom rack and check the area around the drain (I wear medical gloves when doing this). There could be little bits of bone, food particles, paper, etc. that are blocking the drain.

- The spray arms have several holes in them where water sprays out. These can get clogged, but they're easy to clean. Poke the holes carefully with a toothpick and scrub with an old toothbrush dipped in white vinegar.

- Put a small dishwasher-safe bowl on the top rack of the empty dishwasher. Fill the bowl with white vinegar. Run the dishwasher without soap or dishes on the hottest setting.

- After the vinegar wash is finished, sprinkle ½ cup baking soda on the bottom of the empty dishwasher. Run the dishwasher without soap or dishes on the hottest setting.

LIVING ROOM

Sometimes we spend so much time living in the living room, we don't always see what needs to be cleaned. (When was the last time you washed the walls in your living room?) It's important to give your living room or family room a little TLC with some extra cleaning.

These safe, natural cleaning recipes will help you get the whole room clean without nasty chemicals.

Air Freshener Spray

When I see the junk that advertisers try to pass off on us as "pure" or "natural," I have a fit. Because those terms are not regulated, any manufacturer can slap those words on a package and fool the public into thinking a product is safe.

For example, a popular "breezy" air freshener gets a health grade of "C"* from the Environmental Working Group. It may contain ingredients with potential for skin irritation/allergies/damage, acute aquatic toxicity, and chronic aquatic toxicity. Do you want to spray that into the air your family breathes? Me neither.

Here's a natural air freshener spray that's safe for everybody. You can customize the scent any way you like with essential oils.

Ingredients

1 tablespoon baking soda

2 cups distilled or purified water

20 drops essential oil (a single oil, or a combination—see suggestions below)

Supplies

16-ounce spray bottle

Instructions

- Measure the baking soda into a bowl and add the essential oil(s) on top.
- Using a whisk or fork, mix the oil into the baking soda. This will help keep the oil suspended in the water.
- Put the baking soda/essential oil mixture into the spray bottle and top off with the distilled water. Label your bottle, shake before use, and breathe happy—and safely.

---

* "Febreze Air Effects Air Refresher, Linen & Sky Cleaner Rating." EWG. Accessed December 23, 2021. ewg.org/guides/cleaners/5121-FebrezeAirEffectsAirRefresherLinenSky/.

Recommended Scents

- Renew: eight drops lemon essential oil, eight drops orange essential oil, six drops peppermint essential oil

- Fresh & Clean: eight drops lemon essential oil, eight drops lavender essential oil, four drops rosemary essential oil

- Hawaiian Sun: three drops orange essential oil, two drops ginger essential oil, two drops ylang-ylang essential oil

Natural Wall Cleaner

Because different paint finishes need to be cleaned in different ways, always test this in an out-of-the-way spot before using it on the entire wall.

Ingredients

¼ cup unscented liquid castile soap

1½ gallons warm tap water

Supplies

3-gallon or larger bucket

Soft cellulose sponge

Instructions

- Mix the castile soap in the warm water. Use a soft cellulose sponge to gently clean, starting at the top of the wall and working down. Rinse the sponge often in clean water.

Dusting Spray

. . . .

Take the pledge to toss out your lemony-fresh chemical spray and make your own dusting polish! Those yellow spray bottles of furniture polish that we grew up with have a health grade of "D"* from the Environmental Working Group. They contain ingredients that may cause cancer and damage to DNA. Yikes.

This homemade wood polish recipe works best for finished wood, including laminate or veneer surfaces. For unfinished wood, I recommend plain jojoba oil without any added ingredients.

Ingredients

½ cup white vinegar or citrus vinegar

½ cup distilled or purified water

¼ cup jojoba oil

10 drops of lemon or orange essential oil

Supplies

16-ounce spray bottle

Microfiber cloth or old T-shirt

Instructions

- Combine the jojoba oil and essential oil in your spray bottle, and swirl gently to combine. Then add the vinegar and water.

- Close the bottle tightly and label. Shake before using.

To Use

- Instead of spraying this directly onto furniture, I recommend applying a small amount to a microfiber cloth or an old T-shirt. Then use the cloth to gently polish your furniture in a circular motion.

---

* "Pledge Furniture Spray, Lemon Clean Cleaner Rating." EWG. (n.d.). Retrieved January 10, 2022, from ewg.org/guides/cleaners/1395-PledgeFurnitureSprayLemonClean/.

- This way you get a nice, polished surface without any slick residue or oily buildup. If this leaves your furniture too oily, use another cloth to buff away any excess.

Notes

- I like a polish that isn't too heavy on the oil, but you can tweak this recipe if you'd like. You can add more oil or reduce the liquid ingredients to get a thicker, more oil-based polish. If you prefer a thicker polish, then store it in a widemouthed canning jar.

- A lot of natural dusting spray recipes call for olive oil, but I chose jojoba oil for a couple of reasons. Jojoba oil is actually considered a wax rather than an oil. This quality makes it an excellent choice for polishing wood furniture, as it adds a natural protective coating to the wood surface. Because it's also a liquid, it doesn't leave residue like some waxes can.

- Jojoba oil has a very long shelf life of 5 years, which means it's less likely to go rancid over time. Most olive oil has a shelf life of 2–3 years, while other vegetable oils tend to last for 6–18 months.

Carpet Deodorizer

Use this carpet deodorizer anytime you need to neutralize odors or give the room a clean, fresh scent.

Ingredients

1 cup baking soda

10 drops essential oil (a single scent or a combination)

Supplies

Jar with shaker lid (a powdered Parmesan cheese shaker works great)

Instructions

- Put baking soda in a small bowl and add essential oil on top. Mix well with a fork until the oil is completely incorporated.
- Pour into a labeled jar with shaker lid.

To Use

- Sprinkle carpet deodorizer evenly over your entire carpet. Allow to sit for 10–30 minutes, then vacuum thoroughly.

Carpet Stain Remover

Be sure to get to stains as soon as possible! The longer they sit and soak, the more damage they do. Before using this on your carpet, test it in an inconspicuous place.

Mix this recipe up as needed—don't try to store it for later.

Ingredients

1 tablespoon clear liquid dish soap

1 tablespoon white vinegar

2 cups warm tap water

Supplies

16-ounce spray bottle

Instructions

- Before spraying the stain remover, blot up as much of the stain as possible with a clean rag.
- Mix the ingredients in a spray bottle.

To Use

- Spray the stain with the mixture and blot, blot, blot with a clean rag. I confess that I scrub, scrub, scrub when I use this, but my carpet is more than twenty years old.

LIVING ROOM CLEANING TIPS

- Fasten a sock to the handle of your broom and swish it under the couch or TV table. The sock will attract dust and pet hair, so you don't have to move the furniture every time you clean.

- Use the rubber side of a window squeegee to remove pet hair from couches or upholstered chairs. Just pull the squeegee along the fabric and the pet hair will gather into a little roll that you can throw away.

- Clean your TV remote by putting a drop of hand sanitizer on a paper towel and carefully wiping the remote.

- Stop dirt from getting in by placing a floor mat outside your front door and another one inside the front door. This is especially important during rainy weather, when shoes are extra gross and muddy.

- If you have curtains, either vacuum them with the brush attachment or take them down and wash them in the washing machine (check to ensure the fabric can be washed first).

- Knock down cobwebs from your ceiling with a high-nap paint roller on an extension handle.

BATHROOM

The bathroom can often be a breeding ground for germs and mold, so it's important to keep it clean and disinfected. Thankfully, this is easy to do without chemicals that make your eyes water and your lungs burn.

Bathroom Countertop Cleaner

Instructions

- Use All-Purpose Cleaner (page 17) or Granite Cleaner (page 18) for counters, depending on the surface you're cleaning (I make a separate bottle and keep it in the bathroom for easy access).

- Windows, mirrors, and shower doors will be squeaky clean with Glass Cleaner (page 21).

Toilet Surface Cleaner

. . . .

Did you know that most of the germs in the toilet are on the surfaces, not in the toilet bowl? That's why it's important to use a strong, germ-busting cleaner on these surfaces. Tea tree essential oil is perfect for this.

Ingredients

1 cup distilled or purified water

2 tablespoons unscented liquid castile soap

20 drops tea tree essential oil

Supplies

16-ounce spray bottle

Instructions

• Pour the water, castile soap, and essential oil into the spray bottle.

To Use

• Shake gently, and use to clean the toilet seat, lid, and base. Wipe with a clean microfiber cloth.

Toilet Bowl Cleaner

· ·

This cleaning combo is so simple, you don't really need to measure. The baking soda and vinegar combine to foam away dirt, and the tea tree essential oil kills germs.

Ingredients

½ cup baking soda

1 cup white vinegar or citrus vinegar

10 drops tea tree essential oil

Supplies

Toilet brush

Instructions

- Add all ingredients to the toilet bowl and let it sit for 5 minutes. Swish with a toilet brush and you're done!

Copycat Poo-Pourri

· ·

Technically, this is not a cleaner but a public service. Either way you look at it, it's cheaper and just as effective as the fancy store-bought kind.

Ingredients

1 teaspoon vegetable glycerin

1 teaspoon rubbing alcohol

10 drops wintergreen essential oil

5 drops peppermint essential oil

Distilled or purified water

Supplies

2-ounce glass spray bottle

Instructions

- Put the ingredients into the spray bottle in the order listed. After adding the essential oils, fill the bottle with distilled water.

- Label the bottle and set it conspicuously on the bathroom counter. Inform primary offenders of its presence. Make an arrow with Post-it notes if needed.

To Use

- Shake bottle gently.

- Spritz 4–5 sprays into the toilet before sitting down.

- . . . (ahem) . . .

- Flush and wash and be on your way!

Mold & Mildew Removal

Please use caution when cleaning or removing mold. Extended exposure can cause respiratory issues, skin irritation, and other health problems.

I recommend using medical gloves and a mask so you don't breathe in any mold spores, and to wash your hands when you're done cleaning.

This is a two-part recipe—put it together as needed, because it won't store.

Ingredients

Baking soda

1 cup white vinegar or citrus vinegar

1 cup tap water

20 drops lemon essential oil

20 drops tea tree essential oil

Supplies

16-ounce spray bottle

Medical gloves and mask

Scrub brush

Instructions

Part 1

- Mix baking soda and water in a bowl until it makes a paste.

- Put it on the mold spot and let it sit for 15–20 minutes.

Part 2

- Put the vinegar, water, and essential oils in the spray bottle. Put the lid on and swirl gently to combine. Spray this mixture over the baking soda mixture and let it sit for another 15 minutes.

- Put on your gloves and mask and scrub the mold away with the scrub brush.

- Respray the area with the vinegar mixture and leave it to dry (don't rinse).

Tub & Shower Scrub

Ingredients

1 cup baking soda

10 drops lemon essential oil

¼ cup unscented liquid castile soap

1 tablespoon hydrogen peroxide

Distilled or purified water (if needed) to make the proper texture

Supplies

Squeeze bottle (an upcycled ketchup or mustard bottle is perfect)

Instructions

- In a bowl or measuring cup, mix together the baking soda and castile soap. Add the lemon essential oil and hydrogen peroxide. Add a bit of water to thin it if needed and pour it into a squeeze bottle.

- Use this as a powerful cleaner for the bathtub or shower. Don't use it on glass because the baking soda could scratch it. Use the Glass Cleaner recipe (page 21) instead.

Foaming Hand Soap

Our kids love to use foaming hand soap, and until I examined the ingredients I had no idea what kind of stuff was in it. Most brands, even the natural ones, contain artificial colors, preservatives, and sodium chloride. Yes, there is table salt in your liquid soap.

This homemade foaming soap is rich and moisturizing, and you can add any scent you like with essential oils.

Ingredients

⅔ cup distilled or purified water

1 teaspoon vegetable glycerin

⅓ cup unscented liquid castile soap

15 drops essential oil (a single oil, or a combination—see recommendations below)

Supplies

Foaming hand soap dispenser

Instructions

- Pour the water into the soap dispenser, followed by the vegetable glycerin and castile soap.

- Add the essential oil(s) if using. You can use a single oil or a combination of oils.

- Put the top on the dispenser and gently swirl the ingredients together.

Recommended Scents

- Kitchen: 10 drops lemon essential oil, 5 drops rosemary essential oil

- Sleepytime: 9 drops lavender essential oil, 3 drops cedarwood essential oil

- Bright & Fresh: 6 drops peppermint essential oil, 8 drops orange essential oil

Kill Germs without Bleach

It's important to get rid of germs, but I don't like to use bleach—especially because it's been implicated in cases of asthma.[*] But how do you clean thoroughly without it?

Believe it or not, a couple of common household items are amazing at fighting germs without harming you, your kids, or your pets. We use this combo in the bathroom, kitchen, and on doorknobs and light switches.

This combination was identified by a scientist at Virginia Tech. She deliberately contaminated fruits and vegetables with salmonella, shigella, E. coli, then rinsed them with vinegar and/or hydrogen peroxide. Though the hydrogen peroxide performed well on its own, the two sprays applied in order were even more effective.

Ingredients

White vinegar

Hydrogen peroxide

Supplies

Two 16-ounce opaque spray bottles

Instructions

- Fill one spray bottle with white vinegar and label the bottle.
- Fill the second spray bottle with hydrogen peroxide and label the bottle.

---

[*] Joaquín Sastre, Mauro F. Madero, Mar Fernández-Nieto, Beatriz Sastre, Victoria del Pozo, Manuela García-del Potro, and Santiago Quirce. "Airway Response to Chlorine Inhalation (Bleach) among Cleaning Workers with and without Bronchial Hyperresponsiveness." *American Journal of Industrial Medicine*. U.S. National Library of Medicine, April 2011. ncbi.nlm.nih.gov/pubmed/20957677.

To Use

- Spray the vinegar on the surface you want to disinfect. Let it sit for a few minutes, and don't wipe it off.

- Spray the hydrogen peroxide on the surface. Let it dry and again, don't wipe it off.

Notes

- Don't use this combo on granite, marble, or natural stone. Vinegar is acidic and can damage the stone.

- Keep the vinegar and hydrogen peroxide in separate containers. When combined, they form peracetic acid, which will irritate your eyes and lungs—exactly what we're trying to avoid.

BEDROOMS & OFFICE

Is it a bedroom, or is it your office? Maybe it's both. These tips will help keep every part of your bedroom/office/secret hideout clean and fresh.

Computer or Phone Screen Cleaner

If your laptop, tablet, or phone looks like a greasy-fingered octopus has been holding it, this simple cleaner is just the ticket.

Ingredients

2 tablespoons rubbing alcohol

2 tablespoons distilled or purified water

Supplies

2-ounce spray bottle

Instructions

- Mix the rubbing alcohol and water in a clearly labeled spray bottle.

To Use

- Don't spray this cleaner directly on your screen. Instead, spritz a clean cloth and wipe down the screen. You can also use this to clean your keyboard or mouse, but always spray on a cloth, not on the device.

Goop/Sticker Remover

· ·

It never fails—you want to upcycle a jar or get a price tag off a new cup. But the glue just won't seem to come off! Instead of buying a toxic chemical product, use this natural combo to melt the goo away.

Ingredients

2 tablespoons baking soda

5 drops lemon essential oil

Supplies

Paper towel or microfiber cloth

Instructions

- First remove as much of the sticker as you can, so the mixture can soak through to the glue.

- Apply a drop or two of lemon essential oil and smear it around the gluey area with your finger. Then sprinkle baking soda over the top and scrub off with a paper towel. Repeat if needed for stubborn glue.

Linen Mist

. . . .

This delightful linen spray gives an aromatic boost to bedding, clothing, or fabric-covered furniture. It's safe for most fabrics, but you can always test on an inconspicuous spot before using.

Ingredients

½ cup distilled or purified water

3 tablespoons rubbing alcohol

10 drops essential oil (a single oil, or a combination—see suggestions below)

Supplies

8-ounce spray bottle

Instructions

- Combine the rubbing alcohol and essential oils in the spray bottle. Add the filtered water, and swirl gently until fully combined. Label the bottle.

To Use

- Lightly mist your freshly washed linens or pillows. For best results, shake before each use and mist in a wide arc for an even aroma.

Recommended Scents

- Lavender Love: 10 drops lavender essential oil
- Stress Relief: 5 drops frankincense essential oil, 6 drops bergamot essential oil

THE BENEFITS OF AIR-PURIFYING HOUSEPLANTS

- Houseplants are nature's air filters. We all learned in school that plants take in carbon dioxide and produce oxygen, which is part of their air cleaning magic. But did you know that these air-purifying houseplants also remove ground-level ozone from the air? This is an irritating gas formed by a combination of common air pollutants.

- One is an environmental toxin called VOCs (which stands for volatile aromatic compounds). These are released by plastics and are responsible for the famous "new furniture smell" you notice when you get a new carpet or a new office chair. A lot of common building materials release VOCs.

- Another is NOx, or nitrogen oxides. These are produced by vehicle exhaust, kerosene heaters, gas stoves, burning wood, tobacco smoke, and other combustion processes. These are especially common in the winter months when many homes rely on combustive heating processes.

- Other common pollutants include formaldehyde, benzene, trichlorethylene, xylene, ammonia, mold, allergens, and many others.

- All of these pollutants can irritate the respiratory system and cause symptoms like fatigue, foggy thinking, headaches, and dizziness. This is why having indoor plants that clean the air is so important!

- A good rule of thumb is one plant per 100 square feet of space. That usually means one or two plants in offices, bedrooms, and bathrooms. For larger spaces, consider adding three or four plants.

8 INDOOR PLANTS THAT CLEAN THE AIR

There are a lot of amazing houseplants that clean the air, but today I want to narrow it down to a few of the very best. These plants were listed in a NASA report[*] about using indoor plants for air pollution abatement (cool, huh?).

Rubber Tree (*Ficus elastica***)**

- *Basics:* The rubber tree is a large plant that produces tons of oxygen.

- *Toxins Filtered:* mold, bacteria, formaldehyde, VOCs

- *Growing Tips:* needs well-drained soil and lots of indirect sunlight.

Spider Plant (*Chlorophytum comosum***)**

- *Basics:* Spider plants remove chemicals from the air quickly. They're also pet safe!

- *Toxins Filtered:* carbon monoxide, benzene, formaldehyde

- *Growing Tips:* needs some indirect light and medium moisture.

Snake Plant (*Dracaena trifasciata***)**

- *Basics:* Snake plants have long, waxy leaves and are easy to keep alive.

- *Toxins Filtered:* formaldehyde, trichlorethylene, allergens

- *Growing Tips:* needs minimal water and indirect light.

English Ivy (*Hedera helix***)**

- *Basics:* English ivy is highly effective for filtering out toxins in the air. However, this is not a child or pet-friendly plant.

- *Toxins Filtered:* mold, formaldehyde, allergens, benzene

- *Growing Tips:* needs humidity and medium amounts of direct light.

---

[*] "Interior Landscape Plants for Indoor Air Pollution Abatement - NASA Technical Reports Server (NTRS)." NASA. Accessed December 23, 2021. ntrs.nasa.gov/citations/19930073077.

Dragon Tree (*Dracaena marginata***)**

- *Basics: Dracaena* is known for producing lots of daytime oxygen. It also thrives with very little care.
- *Toxins Filtered:* benzene, VOCs, xylene, formaldehyde
- *Growing Tips:* tolerates low light and only needs weekly watering.

Aloe Vera (*Aloe vera***)**

- *Basics:* Aloe vera is easy to grow and can be used for home remedies, too.
- *Toxins Filtered:* carbon monoxide, benzene, formaldehyde
- *Growing Tips:* does best with lots of light and warmth. Mine is in the kitchen on top of the dishwasher.

Tree Philodendron (*Thaumatophyllum bipinnatifidum***)**

- *Basics:* The philodendron thrives with basic care and has large leaves that make it one of the most powerful air-purifying houseplants. However, this is not a good plant if you have kids or pets.
- *Toxins Filtered:* formaldehyde
- *Growing Tips:* needs indirect light and moderate water.

Bamboo Palm (*Chamaedorea seifrizii***)**

- *Basics:* The bamboo palm is leafy, large, and perfect for bathrooms. If it produces berries, discard them immediately—they are highly poisonous.
- *Toxins Filtered:* ammonia, VOCs, formaldehyde, xylene
- *Growing Tips:* tolerates low light, needs warmth and humidity.

Desk Chair Cleaner

....

- Vacuum the fabric with a handheld vacuum or the nozzle attachment for your upright vacuum. If there are any stains on the fabric, use one of the Natural Stain Removers (page 80).

- Spray All-Purpose Cleaner (page 17) on a clean microfiber cloth and wipe down any plastic pieces (armrests, back, base, etc.).

- Clean the wheels or casters with All-Purpose Cleaner (page 17) and a paper towel.

BEDROOM/OFFICE CLEANING TIPS

- **Clean ceiling fan blades:** Grab a pillowcase and slip it over the blade. Wipe gently and the dust will come off inside the pillowcase. You might have to "borrow" pillowcases from a few beds if you have a lot of ceiling fans!

- **Cleaning sculptures and paintings:** If the paint is secure and not flaking off, gently dust with a lambswool duster or soft-bristle paintbrush. Don't use liquids or solvents—leave that to the professionals.

- **Dusting bookshelves, blinds, light fixtures, etc.:** Use a lambswool duster to gently lift the dust away.

LAUNDRY ROOM & PETS

Ahh, the laundry room. This could easily be the stinkiest room in the house, with all the gym clothes and pet supplies. But now that you're a pro at natural cleaning, you just need a few more tips to completely transform this room.

Laundry Detergent

Turn the tide on your laundry routine with this easy recipe. The big orange box we grew up with gets a health rating of "D"[*] from the Environmental Working Group because it contains ingredients that can damage DNA, nervous system, and vision. Oh, and it can also damage the environment through chronic and acute aquatic toxicity. Yuck.

Ingredients

1 bar Fels-Naptha laundry soap

2 cups washing soda

10 drops orange or lemon essential oil

Supplies

Food processor

Large canning jar or other airtight container

Instructions

- Using the food processor's shredding disc, finely grate the entire bar of soap. Change to the chopping blade and add the washing soda and essential oil, then pulse until combined.

To Use

- Store in a clearly labeled container, and use 2 tablespoons per load of laundry.

Note

- Not recommended for high-efficiency (HE) washers

---

[*] "Tide Ultra Powder Detergent, Original Cleaner Rating." EWG. Accessed December 23, 2021. ewg.org/guides/cleaners/1809-TideUltraPowderDetergentOriginal/.

Freshen Stinky Laundry

. . . .

Does your laundry smell sour or musty, even after you've washed it? Here's an easy, natural way to get the bad smells out of your clean laundry.

Ingredients

White vinegar

Baking soda

Instructions

- Wash half the amount of clothes you would normally put in a load. This ensures everything has plenty of room to swish around, get clean, and then get rinsed well.

- Use the hottest water the garments can handle. For me, this is hot water with a cold rinse.

- Fill the fabric softener dispenser with plain white vinegar. If you don't have a dispenser, pour 1 cup in the washer during the rinse cycle.

- Add 1 cup baking soda along with the laundry soap while the washer is filling.

- After the clothes have agitated for a minute or two, turn the washer off and let the clothes soak for about 30 minutes.

- After the soak, turn the washer on and let it finish as normal.

- Get the clothes in the dryer right away (or line-dry them for extra credit and freshness). Enjoy your fresh, fluffy laundry!

Note

- This works best with top-loading washing machines. If you have a front-load machine or a water-saving machine, soak the clothes in the bathtub with the baking soda. Squeeze them out and put them in the washer with the vinegar to complete the process.

NATURAL STAIN REMOVERS

These stain-remover recipes are broken down by stain type. I've picked a few of the most common stains based on how they need to be removed. For instance, wine and grease are totally different stains and need very different stain remover recipes.

Remember to check the washing instructions for your clothing items before trying these. For special fabrics or dry-clean-only clothing, these methods might not be safe to try.

COFFEE, TEA, OR TOMATO SAUCE

The tannins in coffee, tea, and tomato sauce make these stains unique. But they can be removed if you work quickly.

Ingredients

Baking soda

Unscented liquid castile soap

Instructions

- For tomato sauce, scrape any excess sauce off with the flat end of a butter knife first.

- Act quickly and flush the stain out with cold water.

- Apply a paste of baking soda and castile soap. Allow this to sit for 3–5 minutes.

- Gently rub the fabric together and then soak in cold water for 30 minutes. Then gently rub again to see if the stain is gone.

- Soak in warm water and gently rub the fabric to loosen up any remaining stain particles.

- This should do the trick, but you can repeat the process again for deeper stain removal.

RED WINE OR FRUIT JUICE

First, try to get to the stain as quickly as possible. The longer it sits, the more difficult it becomes to remove. Blot the stain with a clean, dry cloth to remove as much liquid as possible.

Ingredients

Club soda

Table salt

White vinegar

Instructions

- Stretch the clothing over a bowl. Then flush the stain out with cold club soda. (This works better than water.)
- Then pour a generous amount of table salt over the stain and let it sit for 5 minutes.
- Rinse the salt away with warm or very hot water (depending on what's safe for the fabric).
- If some of the stain remains, dab with a 50/50 mixture of warm water and white vinegar. Let it soak for 30 minutes and then launder as usual.

GREASE, SWEAT, OR GRIME

Grease, grime, and sweat make for hard-to-remove stains. But they aren't impossible to remove if you use the right natural stain removers.

Ingredients

Unscented liquid castile soap

Hydrogen peroxide

Baking soda

Instructions

- Make a 50/50 mixture of castile soap and hydrogen peroxide. Then, add enough baking soda to make a thin paste.
- Apply generously to the stain and work it into the fabric with a soft toothbrush.
- Let this sit for 30–60 minutes.
- Launder as usual. Check before drying to see if the stain is fully removed. If not, repeat the process.

MAKEUP, LIPSTICK, INK, PEN, OR MARKER

Makeup and ink are heavily pigmented and can cause serious stains. Don't give up hope! Use these steps to get these tough stains out.

Ingredients

Rubbing alcohol

Table salt

Baking soda

Unscented liquid castile soap

Instructions

- Scrape off any excess with the flat end of a butter knife if needed.
- Soak the end of a sponge in rubbing alcohol. Dab at the remaining stain to remove as much pigment as possible.
- Rinse the sponge and reapply alcohol as needed to prevent spreading the stain.
- Sprinkle a 50/50 mixture of table salt and baking soda on the stain. Dab with a wet cloth until the mixture is gone. Repeat if needed.
- If some staining remains, saturate the stain with castile soap. Leave for 30–60 minutes, then wash in cold water.

Dryer Sheets

· ·

Bounce that box of conventional dryer sheets into the trash and make your own with this easy recipe. Dryer sheets are loaded with harmful chemicals and fragrances, earning them a health grade of "F"* from the Environmental Working Group.

These homemade dryer sheets are great for those of us with sensitive skin. The vinegar helps reduce static cling, and you can customize the scent any way you'd like with essential oils.

Ingredients

1 cup white vinegar

20 drops lemon, orange, or lavender essential oil

Supplies

4" squares of cotton/flannel cloth (old T-shirts or flannel sheets are perfect)

Large widemouthed glass jar with lid

Instructions

- Mix the vinegar and essential oils in the glass jar.

- Fold or roll the fabric squares so they fit into the jar and you can easily remove one or two at a time (i.e., don't just mash them all into the jar).

- Close the lid and flip the jar upside down a few times to ensure all the fabric squares are wet.

- To use, pull one or two fabric squares out of the jar and squeeze to remove excess liquid. Toss in the dryer along with your clean clothes.

---

* "Bounce Dryer Sheets, Fresh Linen Cleaner Rating." EWG. Accessed December 23, 2021. ewg.org/guides/cleaners/5433-BounceDryerSheetsFreshLinen/.

How to Clean Your Washing Machine

FRONT-LOAD WASHER

Ingredients

2 cups white vinegar or citrus vinegar

⅓ cup baking soda

Hydrogen peroxide

Supplies

16-ounce spray bottle

Microfiber cleaning cloth

Old toothbrush

Instructions

- Spray vinegar on the gasket at the front of the machine. Be sure any folds or nooks and crannies are thoroughly sprayed.

- Sprinkle some baking soda on your cleaning cloth and scrub all surfaces of the gasket carefully. You may want to use an old toothbrush to scrub any tight spots.

- If you see mold on the gasket, spray hydrogen peroxide on it after you're done scrubbing.

- Wipe down the top and front of the washer, the knobs, and any other areas with All-Purpose Cleaner (page 17) or vinegar. Remove and clean the detergent drawer, too.

- Finally, pour 2 cups of white vinegar into the detergent dispenser and ⅓ cup baking soda into the drum of the machine. Then run the cleaning cycle.

(continued)

TOP-LOAD WASHER

Ingredients

White vinegar

Baking soda

Supplies

16-ounce spray bottle

Microfiber cleaning cloth

Old toothbrush

Instructions

- Set your washer to run a large load with hot water. Don't add clothes or laundry detergent. As it's filling with water, add 4 cups of white vinegar.

- When the washer starts to agitate, add 1 cup of baking soda. Allow it to run for a few seconds to mix the baking soda in (it will bubble and fizz).

- Turn off the washer and let it sit for at least 30 minutes.

- Wipe down the top and front of the washer, the knobs, and any other areas with All-Purpose Cleaner (page 17) or vinegar.

- Turn the washer back on and let it run through the rest of the cycle. For added cleaning, run another cycle with hot water only (no clothes, detergent, vinegar, or baking soda).

All-Natural Dog Shampoo

· ·

Many animal shampoos have fragrances that smell lovely to us but can completely over-whelm a dog's nose. Dogs have up to 300 million smell receptors (we have about 6 million), so all those botanical extracts and essential oils are like pouring straight perfume on your pup. This easy recipe is gentle on your doggie's nose and still cleans well.

Ingredients

¼ cup unscented liquid castile soap

¾ cup distilled or purified water

Supplies

Squeeze bottle (a recycled ketchup bottle is perfect for this)

Instructions

- Combine water and soap in squeeze bottle and swirl gently to combine. Label the bottle.

To Use

- Massage into your dog's coat and rinse thoroughly.

Dog Toy Cleaning Spray

I admit that I never thought about cleaning dog toys—but if you take toys or balls to the park, you never know what gets on them. This easy spray will help remove the mystery gunk.

Ingredients

2 tablespoons unscented liquid castile soap

1½ cups distilled or purified water

Supplies

16-ounce spray bottle

Instructions

• Pour the water and castile soap into the spray bottle and label the bottle.

To Use

• Shake gently before use, and spray heavily on toys. Then rinse and allow to air-dry. This is not for use on battery-operated toys!

NATURAL FLOOR CLEANERS

I know, I know. Nobody likes mopping the floor every week. But if you don't mop, the dirt will wear the shine off your floor like sandpaper.

The key to easy and effective mopping is to use two buckets—one for washing and one for rinsing. That way you aren't mopping with dirty water or wasting water and soap by emptying and refilling a single bucket.

I like traditional wringer mops because you can control the amount of soapy water you use. It's lightweight and better for scrubbing than string mops, too.

Tile or Wood Floor Cleaner

. . . .

Ingredients

2 buckets filled with 3 gallons warm water each

Add ¼–½ cup unscented liquid castile soap to one of the buckets

Instructions

- Dip your mop into the soapy water bucket, squeeze out the excess water, and mop a small area. Then rinse the mop in the plain water bucket, wring it out, and go back to the soapy water bucket.

- Change the rinse water if it gets dirty. No need to rinse the floor after mopping.

Vinyl Floor Cleaner

Ingredients

2 buckets filled with 3 gallons warm water each

Add 3 cups apple cider vinegar or citrus vinegar to one of the buckets, plus 5 drops liquid dish soap if the floor is very dirty

Instructions

- Dip your mop into the vinegar water bucket, squeeze out the excess water, and mop a small area. Then rinse the mop in the plain water bucket, wring it out, and go back to the vinegar water bucket.

- Change the rinse water if it gets dirty. If you're using dish soap, give the floor a quick mop with clean water to finish.

RESOURCES

Congratulations! You have everything you need to clean your home naturally, spending less money, using fewer products, without breathing in dangerous chemicals.

Visit brownthumbmama.com/non-toxic-home for lots more information on how to detox your home, your skincare products, and much more.

See my favorite home and gardening products at my Amazon store: amazon.com/shop/brownthumbmama.

ABOUT BROWN THUMB MAMA

BrownThumbMama.com is a very special corner of the internet for people who see the world a little differently.

- Maybe you're tired of disposable living, Styrofoam cups, and plastic bags.
- Maybe you want to grow a few vegetables instead of relying on the store.
- Maybe you'd like to learn about natural ways to improve your health.
- Maybe you're interested in cooking your favorite foods from scratch.

Welcome home . . . you're in the right place.

Brown Thumb Mama makes natural living easy. Whether you need simple recipes, gardening tips, sustainability ideas, or herbal remedies, there's something here for you.

What Is Natural Living?

Natural living does *not* mean you have to give away everything you own, stop wearing makeup, and live in a stone hut.

Natural living means:

- Respecting the Earth and her inhabitants
- Making sustainable choices whenever possible
- Doing our best and improving every day
- Making small changes toward green and conscious living.

Some of us make natural cleaners and shop at the farmers' market. Some of us ride bikes or walk instead of using cars.

Some of us pack lunches in reusable containers instead of plastic bags. Some of us have downsized our homes or live in conscious communities.

All of these things are great! No matter where you are on your natural living journey, **you are welcome here.**

ABOUT THE AUTHOR

I first learned the principles of "leave no trace" in high school, when I took trips hiking, canoeing, and backpacking in California with friends. Each summer we'd go on a new adventure, carrying our gear on our backs and packing out all of our trash.

We camped at Point Reyes National Seashore, hiked up to a fire lookout in the Sierra Buttes, and finished our adventures by summiting Mount Whitney before leaving for college.

When hiking in the backcountry, our motto was "take only pictures and leave only footprints."

At the time, I didn't realize that this was causing a change in my mindset. But as I got older, these ecological concepts stuck with me.

When we got married and had a family, I didn't want to raise our children on fast food and TV dinners. I wanted them to know the cycles of nature and to help take care of their planet.

Even though we lived in the city, we made sustainable choices whenever we could. I started growing vegetables in our front and back yards, baking my own bread, and shopping at thrift stores.

Books like *Radical Homemakers* and *Making Home* showed me that I wasn't alone in making these changes.

I created Brown Thumb Mama to share my natural living journey, and to help you live a greener life. Some people think it's weird, and that's fine. This is a place for the rest of us.

You're marching to the beat of a different drummer? Good. I am, too.

Let's go change the world.

CONVERSION CHART

If you're accustomed to using metric measurements, I don't want you to be inconvenienced by the imperial measurements I use in this book.

Weight (Dry Ingredients)

1 oz		30 g
4 oz	¼ lb	120 g
8 oz	½ lb	240 g
12 oz	¾ lb	360 g
16 oz	1 lb	480 g
32 oz	2 lb	960 g

Volume (Liquid Ingredients)

½ tsp.		2 ml
1 tsp.		5 ml
1 Tbsp.	½ fl oz	15 ml
2 Tbsp.	1 fl oz	30 ml
¼ cup	2 fl oz	60 ml
⅓ cup	3 fl oz	80 ml
½ cup	4 fl oz	120 ml
⅔ cup	5 fl oz	160 ml
¾ cup	6 fl oz	180 ml
1 cup	8 fl oz	240 ml
1 pt	16 fl oz	480 ml
1 qt	32 fl oz	960 ml

Length

¼ in	6 mm
½ in	13 mm
¾ in	19 mm
1 in	25 mm
6 in	15 cm
12 in	30 cm

INDEX

tea, 80

NOTES

NOTES

NOTES

NOTES

NOTES

NOTES